AMERICAN HISTORY

Companion Text

AMERICAN HISTORY

HERON
BOOKS

Published by
Heron Books, Inc.
20950 SW Rock Creek Road
Sheridan, OR 97378

heronbooks.com

―――――――――――

Special thanks to all the teachers and students who
provided feedback instrumental to this edition.

―――――――――――

Fourth Edition © 2005, 2023 Heron Books
All Rights Reserved

ISBN 978-0-89-739351-5

22 October 2023

LEARNING
at the
SPEED
of
You

At Heron Books, we think learning should be engaging and fun. It should be hands-on and allow students to move at their own pace.

To facilitate this we have created a learning guide that will help any student progress through this book, chapter by chapter, with confidence and interest.

Get learning guides at
heronbooks.com/learningguides.

For teacher resources,
such as a final exam, email
teacherresources@heronbooks.com.

We would love to hear from you!
Email us at *feedback@heronbooks.com.*

CONTENTS

6 CHECKS AND BALANCES AS ESTABLISHED BY THE U.S. CONSTITUTION 41

7 NOTES ON THE FILM *THE DAY AFTER TRINITY* 47

APPENDIX 55

CHAPTER 1

WELCOME TO AMERICAN HISTORY

CHAPTER 1

WELCOME TO AMERICAN HISTORY

As you probably already know, **history** is the subject that deals with the lives of groups of people, whether large or small, of where they came from, where they got to, and the things they made and did along the way. Whether written down or passed on as spoken tales, it is a record of what happened in the past.

History isn't just a set of facts to be learned. It is the story of past adventures, challenges, disasters and victories. It gives you ideas, individuals and events to think about and to compare with current events, the world around you, and your own ideas, interests and goals.

The American history courses will take you from prehistory—the time before people began to write down the things they did—to the present day. Along the way you will find stories of heroism, curiosity, survival, evil and good.

As you study, you will be invited to actively investigate the ideas, individuals and events presented in these courses and come to your own conclusions about them.

Let's get started!

CHAPTER 2

HISTORY, MAPS AND TIME LINES

CHAPTER 2

HISTORY, MAPS AND TIME LINES

Reporters, police detectives and other researchers sometimes use a system called the Six W's (even though one "W" is really an "H") to make sure they're not leaving anything out of a key report:

Who was involved?

What happened?

Where did it happen?

Why did it happen?

When did it happen?

How did it happen?

In our reporting of history and in understanding what others have reported, we're concerned with the same Six W's.

History is made by people, their actions and their ideas. History isn't over; everything we do every day is part of the history of our time. The people in history, whether "important" or not, are the ones who direct the continuing story of humankind—where it's been, where it is now, and where it's going. People and the ideas that guide them make up the *who* of our Six W's.

But people and ideas aren't quite enough by themselves to be called history. People and ideas affect events, and are in turn affected by events. An **event** can be defined as "a happening or occurrence, especially when important." A historical event is one that we feel is important to the plot of the big story. It helps to show who we are and how we got that way. Knowing the *who,* we can describe an event by telling *what* happened, *how* it happened and *why* it happened.

When we read fiction or watch a movie for entertainment, the *where* and the *when* are often not very important. The stories could be taking place anywhere or at any time, and it doesn't much matter. But in history, it does matter. History is about real people doing real things in real places at real times. Place and time are key points for properly appreciating history.

Many students of history find that when they start to fully nail down those two points—the *where* and *when* of a particular event—they have an easier time understanding and remembering the other four W's also. That's where maps and time lines come in.

MAPS

Finding the place you're reading about on a map or a globe increases your understanding considerably, and your textbook includes many good maps for that reason.

You can also make your own maps. If you go so far as to make a free-hand map of the area you are studying, chances are that you'll have an easier time remembering it. You can also mark place names on an outline map, like this one of North America. It has been shrunk from the online version to save space, but of course you would want a much larger copy to work with.

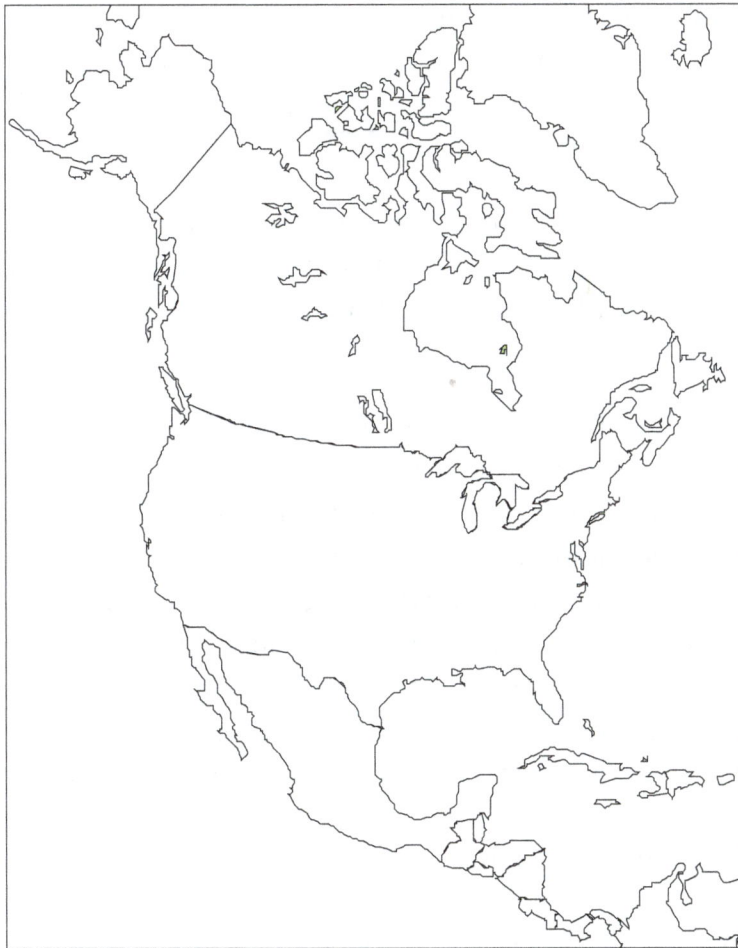

Maps are an indispensable tool for studying history, so you will be doing a lot of map work on these American history courses.

TIME LINES

Some people think history is all about memorizing a lot of dates, and it is true that you will find it helpful to know a few key dates. Knowing the date of an event helps you keep track of the story.

For instance, everyone should know that the U.S. Declaration of Independence was signed in 1776. If you realize that the Declaration of Independence happened *after* a long series of disagreements between the Americans of that day and the British government, and you know also that it came *before* some of the main battles of the American Revolution, you have already put a great deal of organization into the data you are studying. You have established how that event relates to other events.

To help with that kind of organization, a good tool to use is a diagram called a time line. A **time line** is a line with dates marked on it, notes about important events, and sometimes illustrations. Below you can see an example of a time line.

On that time line, find the time marked **0**. This is certainly not the beginning of history, but since we have to start somewhere, it is convenient to call some year "Year 0." A group in Europe decided to start dating time from the birth of Jesus of Nazareth (the founder of the Christian religion), so **0** is supposed to be the year of his birth. Jesus was called the "**Christ**"—a name which means the "Chosen One of God," so the time before the birth of Christ was called **B.C.** or **BC** (Before Christ). Time after the birth of Christ was labeled **A.D.** or **AD** for *Anno Domini*—a Latin phrase that means "in the year of the Lord," or years after Christ's birth. In books written more recently, you will often see these written as **B.C.E.** or **BCE** (Before the Common Era or Before the Christian Era) and **C.E.** or **CE** (Common Era or Christian Era).

On the time line, you can see a few dates and a few events as examples to show one way to make a time line.

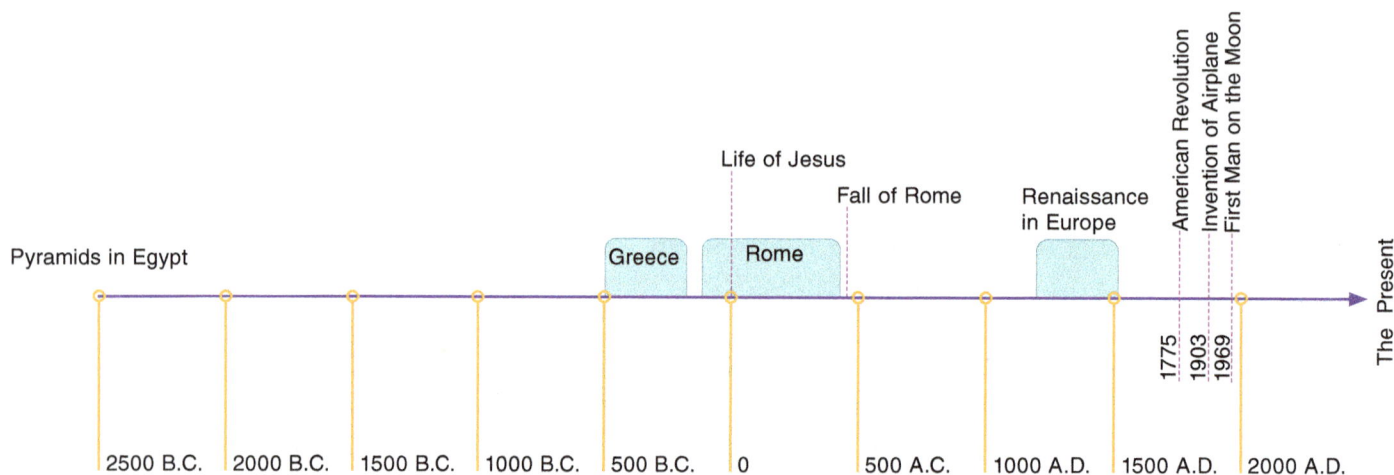

BEFORE COLUMBUS

CHAPTER 3

BEFORE COLUMBUS

Many people say that Columbus discovered America, but that is not really true.

When Columbus arrived, millions of Native Americans were already living in North and South America, and had been for many thousands of years.

In fact, some historians think that there were about four million Native Americans in the area now called the United States and Canada, and seventeen million in the area now called Mexico. There were many different groups, each with their own language and way of life.

Let's take a look at some of these groups.

NATIVE AMERICANS OF THE UNITED STATES AND CANADA

Northwest Coast

This is a narrow area of land on the West Coast from southern Alaska down to northern California. The climate was mild and the land was covered by forests, so there were many animals and plants for food. There were rivers and the Pacific Ocean nearby, so many of the people fished, and salmon was a large part of their diet.

The people generally lived in large houses made of logs. In Alaska, Canada and Washington they used cedar logs to carve and paint large, colorful totem poles.

In Oregon and California, they did not make totem poles, possibly because they did not have the right kind of wood for carving.

Southwest

The Southwest was much hotter and drier than the Northwest coast, so plants didn't grow as well.

The Native Americans of the Southwest learned how to farm with very little water. They grew corn, squash and beans in small fields. They also hunted deer and antelope.

In some places, they built large buildings out of sun-dried clay bricks, called **adobe**. These buildings were made up of many apartments and storage rooms. The Native Americans of the Southwest were very good artists and weavers.

The Great Basin and Plateau

The land in Nevada and some other western states forms a "basin" between the Sierra Nevada and the Rocky Mountains, called the **Great Basin**.

The Great Basin is mostly desert. It takes up most of Nevada and Utah, and smaller parts of California, Idaho, Oregon and Wyoming. The people there lived in small groups and moved about in search of food.

To the north was higher land where the climate was a little wetter and where there were more plants and animals. People there lived by hunting and trapping the deer, elk and antelope.

California

The largest number of Native Americans in the United States lived west of the Sierra Nevada Mountains in what is now California. The weather was mild and there was plenty of food.

The people ate roots, acorns from oak trees, and gathered shellfish from the edge of the Pacific Ocean. For the most part, life was peaceful and easygoing for them.

The Plains

The plains were mostly grasslands stretching for hundreds and hundreds of miles. The grasslands provided food for herds of bison which numbered in the millions. The people hunted the bison for meat. They used the hides for making clothes and coverings for their cone-shaped tents, called **teepees.**

Before the 1500s, the Plains people traveled and hunted on foot. When the Spanish came to explore the plains in the 1500s, they traveled on horses brought from Europe. Some of the horses escaped and were captured by the native people in the area.

Using horses, the people of the plains could hunt bison much easier. If they needed to follow the bison herds, they could pack up and carry their belongings on the horses.

Eastern Woodlands

The Native Americans of the East lived in forests where the climate was good and rainfall was plentiful, and there were many lakes and rivers.

There were many wild plants and animals for food, but they also became good farmers. The eastern people used wood to make their homes, and most of them lived in permanent villages. They also made canoes and used them to travel long distances on water.

The Arctic and Tundra

The native people of the far north had to learn how to live with year-round snow and ice, and very cold weather. They survived by hunting seal, whales, fish and caribou. They were good inventors—they invented igloos, snow goggles, sledges and kayaks.

Forests of Canada and Alaska

There was another Native American group that lived in the forests of Alaska and throughout most of Canada. In this cold, broad region, the people lived mainly on elk, caribou, deer and fish.

MEXICO, CENTRAL AND SOUTH AMERICA

There were many more Native Americans living in Mexico, Central and South America. The two main groups were the Aztecs and the Incas. They built large cities and lived quite differently from the northern Native Americans.

When the Europeans arrived, the Aztecs lived in the lands that are now part of central Mexico. The Incas lived in the Andes Mountains of South America from Chile to Ecuador.

The Aztecs and Incas built cities and road systems through the mountains, developed an accurate calendar, and made advances in medicine.

There was an earlier large Native American civilization called the Maya, but it disappeared 600 years before the Europeans came, and no one knows exactly why.

The Mayans lived in lands that are now part of southern Mexico and Central America. They built big cities and developed art, science, medicine and mathematics. The ancestors of many of the people now living in Central America were Mayans.

CHAPTER 4

HISTORY RESEARCH AND PRESENTATIONS

CHAPTER 4

HISTORY
RESEARCH AND
PRESENTATIONS

WHY RESEARCH HISTORY?

History is the story of the human race on this planet, and right now that's the biggest story we have. We research history—American history, in this case—because we want to understand how we ended up where we are today, and how we as individuals are connected to that story.

The truth is, we are connected in all sorts of ways.

We are connected through the groups we are part of. For better or worse, both Americans and non-Americans have been influenced tremendously by the story of America, by the ideas it has stood for, both good and bad, and by the ways in which it has or has not lived up to its early promise. America and Americans have in turn been influenced by every nation, race and religious group in the world.

We are connected to the story through our families. Most Americans, whether Native Americans, or European or African or Asian Americans, had family members who had to confront all sorts of hardships—and live through all sorts of interesting adventures—in order to come to this country. Your families are contributing to American history right now, and are being influenced by it in return.

And no matter your age, you yourself as an individual are already a part of American history. What you do right here and now every day, no matter how small, is going into our story.

We study history and research history in order to understand what has happened in the past, not just as a collection of facts, but as a real *story*. We want to understand the characters and their ideas, where they came from, what they did, when that was, and how and why they did what they did. We want to know what mistakes the characters made, and how they might have done better. All of that goes to make up the plot of the story.

Once we really know what's been going on, we can find ourselves becoming more and more interested in how each of the episodes comes out—including the episodes we're living right now.

RESEARCH IS DETECTIVE WORK

Detective stories are sometimes called "whodunits" (who-done-its) because the detective is trying to solve the mystery of a crime.

Remember the "six W's" of detective work (who, what, where, why, when and how)? Detectives are just like other researchers, historians and reporters in trying to establish those six W's, starting with the what (the crime itself). In addition to finding the identity of the criminal (the who), they always have to demonstrate the criminal's *method* (how was the crime done?) and *motive* (why was it done?).

History research is no different, but in history we research not just the historical crimes (though there are certainly lots of those!) but also, more importantly, the great things people have done in the world, and the great people who have done them. There are still many mysteries about history, mysteries that can be solved by anyone who has the patience to do some digging around, asking questions and trying to figure out how all the pieces go together.

In this course, no one is asking you to discover things no one has thought of before. But you will certainly be expected to discover things *you* never knew about before, and to put different facts together in ways you never connected them before. That's the exciting part of history research.

A simple research project may involve taking just one fact or idea that you want to find out about, finding a few other facts that are connected with it, and assembling those into a better picture of the subject than you had before.

For example, suppose you had read a little bit about how the Native Americans came to North America. You might then want to know something about where the different tribes wound up after that. You could check a reference or two for the information you want. To present your research, you could download or print a blank outline map of North America, and add captions and representative pictures of the tribes in their respective locations. This would be a perfectly fine simple research project that might take half an hour or so.

If you want to do a slightly larger research project, you might focus on a single tribe and combine a short research report with a visual presentation. Here is an example:

RESEARCH ON THE CHIPPEWA TRIBE

The Chippewa are one of the biggest tribes of the Algonquian family. There are about 200,000 Chippewa today, most of them still living in their original territories in the north-central United States and southern Canada.

Tribal names

Chippewa (in the U.S.): means "puckering" because their moccasins are puckered

Ojibway, Ojibwa, Ojibwe (Canada): a variation of the same word as "Chippewa"

Anishinabe (what the Chippewa call themselves): "original people"

Facts of Interest

"The Ojibwe people were less devastated by European epidemics than their densely populated Algonquian cousins to the east, and they resisted manhandling by the whites much better."

(http://www.native-languages.org/chippewa.htm).

"There are nearly 150 different bands of Chippewa Indians living throughout their original home land in the northern United States (especially Minnesota, Wisconsin and Michigan), and southern Canada (especially Ontario, Manitoba and Saskatchewan)."

(http://bigorrin.org/chippewa_kids.htm).

RESEARCH AND PRESENTATION

Your own projects are limited only by your imagination—and your willingness to be a historical detective!

A research project really has two main parts:

1) the research (where do you get your information?), and

2) the presentation (how will you display your results?).

In these American History courses, you are encouraged to try as many kinds of research as possible in order to get experience with more than one. Here are some possibilities:

- A regular encyclopedia, such as *The World Book* or *The Book of Knowledge*.

- Specialized reference books, such as *The Young Reader's Companion to American History*, edited by John A. Garraty, or *Discovering America's Past*, published by *Reader's Digest*.

- Portions of your textbooks that you haven't been assigned to read.

- Videos on historical topics (if approved by your academic supervisor).

- Online websites (see the list of recommended websites at the end of the chapter).

- Personal interviews with parents, grandparents or older people in your area—about your own family tree, for instance.

- Visits to museums, historical societies or historical locations in your area.

You can also do different types of presentations on what you find out from your research. Here are some possibilities:

1. A simple visual presentation, whether hand-drawn or done on the computer.

2. A written research report of your own (not just a printout from online).

3. Combination of research report and visual presentation.

4. An artistic project, such as a painting, poem, song, model, skit, historical fiction short story, etc.

5. A complete, well-organized essay. This one is required once on each of the four courses of American History.

6. A 3- to 5-minute oral presentation from notes, including some type of visual presentation (required once on each American History course).

7. A digital slides presentation, such as PowerPoint.

In any presentation, don't forget the six W's. You are not absolutely required to include all six in every presentation, but you should make sure you aren't ignoring crucial information, either in your research or in your presentation.

One last thing about history research: Have fun with it. It *is* fun!

RECOMMENDED RESEARCH WEBSITES

Browsing the internet for research information can sometimes get you into material that is too advanced for your current level of history knowledge. Here is a list of interesting websites at the proper level for American History 1–4.

http://www.historymatters.gmu.edu

From the website's home page: "Designed for high school and college teachers and students, *History Matters* serves as a gateway to web resources and offers other useful materials for teaching U.S. history."

The section "Many Pasts"

(<http://historymatters.gmu.edu/browse/manypasts/) contains many fascinating **primary documents**. These are materials written by the people who actually experienced first-hand the events we can otherwise view only through the eyes of those who create our history texts, films, etc.

http://www.firstpeople.us/

Good site for information on Native American tribes.

http://historyforkids.org/

This website was designed for Middle School, but it has excellent history data.

http://images.google.com/

This is an excellent way to find images for a time line or research presentation.

http://smplanet.com/imperialism/toc.html

When you get to the late-19th century, you will find that the U.S. was expanding into new territories in different ways. The people who created this website don't think that was ethical. You can make up your own mind about that, but the material here is very interesting, including some great pictures.

CHAPTER 5

PERSPECTIVES ON HISTORY

CHAPTER 5

PERSPECTIVES ON HISTORY

A **perspective** is a point of view or way of looking at things, ideas, people or events.

For example, a soccer player has a different perspective on a game than a referee; they don't look at it or see it the same way, even though it's the same game. They see it and think about it differently.

Perspective is also how a person sees things in relation to each other. A farmer might be happy for rain. It waters the crops and gives the animals a drink. A family planning a picnic might have a very different perspective. The rain ruined their plans. They have different views about the rain.

And this is what perspective has to do with history. People can look at the same people, ideas and events in history and see different connections or relationships, depending on their background, their education, their religious beliefs and many other things. You might expect, for instance, that twin brothers who were raised and educated together would grow up having the same perspective on things, and they might. But they might not. Individuals don't always see things the same way.

Do you think the soccer player would describe exactly the same game as the referee? They both might relate facts, but they saw the game from different perspectives, so the "history" of the game as told by these two different people might sound like two different histories, even like two different games! Is one of them more true than the other? Should we believe the player because they were in the action, or the referee because they were watching both sides closely?

In history, this means that there can be two very different perspectives on why a war started or which scientific discoveries were most influential in a particular place and time. More often, there are several different perspectives.

HOW DOES PERSPECTIVE MAKE A DIFFERENCE?

Have you ever read about something that happened in the past and wondered what you would have done if you had been alive at that time? If you weren't sure, it may have been because you simply didn't understand the event well enough to make a decision about it.

On the other hand, maybe you read about some other event in the past and felt certain you did know how you would have acted—but then you got more information and realized that your earlier opinion was based on incomplete information, possibly from only one side of an issue.

That can happen when you study history. As you come to understand more, you often find your ideas changing, frequently more than once, as you discover new things. Each time you do that, you gain a new, more intelligent perspective, and your ideas about it become more valuable.

How we view past problems and their solutions, and how well we truly understand them, enables us to look at similar problems in the present, and to decide how those things should be solved right now.

Suppose we were doing our best to be responsible citizens and help to solve the problems of the world, yet we had an entirely false understanding—a false perspective—of what the real problems were, and of what was causing them. The result, of course, would be poor decisions and problems not solved. We might also pass on our false ideas to others. We would possibly elect leaders who would agree with our wrong ideas and spread them further, and make more poor decisions affecting even more people badly.

TYPES OF HISTORICAL (AND POLITICAL) PERSPECTIVE

Politics has to do with the activities involved in governing a country, state or other area. People often have different ideas about what a government should be trying to do. This affects their views about things like what laws should exist, who should have rights, what responsibilities people have, and how they should be treated. It can also affect their views on historical events.

Historical perspective is nearly always closely related to *political* perspective, so to discuss one is to discuss the other at the same time. In the United States at this time there are several main types of ideas about how history is to be understood and applied to real life. Each of these types has many variations, but for right now let's look only at a few of the major categories.

These ideas are often thought of as being arranged on a scale that runs from left to right. The following descriptions are typical of those we classify very roughly as "Left," "Right" and "Middle of the Road."[1]

Since we're talking about a scale, however, there are many, many differences of opinion as groups and individuals move from left to right, or right to left. But most people have certain ways of looking at life that fall loosely into these three broad categories:

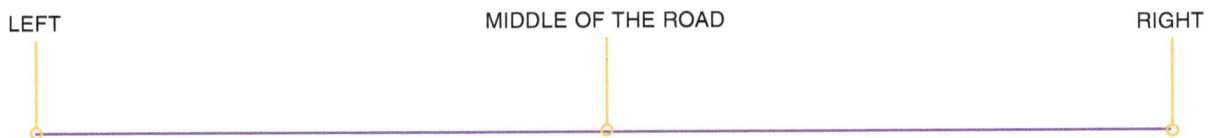

LEFT	MIDDLE OF THE ROAD	RIGHT

LEFT: In the United States today, people on the "left" tend to think of history as a struggle between groups of people who have come out on top in society by

---

1 Note: A tremendous amount of research and discussion went into the information and ideas presented here. A list of the references used is included in the back of the book. The intention has been to make this chapter as accurate and as fair to different perspectives as it could possibly be.

dominating and taking advantage of others, and other groups that have more often come out on the bottom, or at least lower on the social ladder.

A successful group may be called "privileged," or "advantaged." Similarly, a less successful group can be referred to as "underprivileged" or "disadvantaged."

People on the "left" often express compassion for those who are thought of as members of minority groups because they believe these people couldn't really do anything about being born into that situation. They think that many of those on top in society have gotten where they are by looking out for their own well-being, acting in a primarily selfish or greedy way.

Many people on the "left" think of themselves as members of one or more minorities. Others on the left are members of a more dominant group who believe they can improve conditions for everyone by taking sides with those on the bottom. They believe that government should play an important role in helping minorities, including making the rest of society assist in that effort. They favor the idea that all citizens should be far more equal than they are in terms of how much wealth and power each person is able to control.

In the United States today, people on the political left are called **liberal, left-wing** or **progressive**. The largest official group representing people on the left is the **Democratic Party**.

A good example of a history textbook with a "left" perspective is *A Young People's History of the United States* by Howard Zinn, which you will have an opportunity to use in some of your research.

RIGHT: Those on the "right" end of the political scale usually believe that people who are the most successful are successful because they are more able to understand and apply the laws of nature (*natural law*), or of a Supreme Being or higher idea of some sort. They may consider themselves to be more religious than those on the left, who are often suspicious of religion, particularly of traditional religions.

Many people on the right believe that human beings have free will, rather than being controlled by forces outside themselves. Therefore, they think that if people aren't successful in life, it is more likely that they are simply making wrong decisions rather than thinking that other groups and individuals are taking advantage of them.

Many on the right fear that private individuals, as well as state and local governments, are in danger of losing important rights and liberties as the national government gains in strength and power, as it has done steadily almost throughout American history.

In recent years, however, many on the right have decided that big government is simply a fact of life, and may not be a problem after all. They agree with the left that government should be strong and active, but they want government to pursue a different set of purposes. They usually think the U.S. should have a more powerful military than it does, for instance, and that national policies should promote big business more than they do, while decreasing the amount we spend on social welfare.

In the United States today, people on the right are often labeled **right-wing** or **conservative**. People on the right who believe in big government are often called **neoconservatives** (*neo-* means "new"). The largest official group representing people on the right is the **Republican Party**.

An example of a history textbook with a "right" perspective is *The Politically Incorrect Guide to American History*,[2] by Thomas E. Woods, Jr. You will be invited to use that book later.

---

2 The term **politically correct** is used to describe a set of opinions, viewpoints and language that is approved by most liberals and, at least in part, disapproved by most conservatives. It was originally used in a more or less joking way by conservatives making fun of those liberal leaders who insisted, in the view of conservatives, that only one particular set of ideas ("correct" ideas) should be allowed free expression. In addition, these liberal leaders were considered to be overly sensitive about words that might be offensive to certain minority groups. For example, liberals would favor the term "hearing impaired" instead of "deaf" in describing someone who couldn't hear, or the term "CE" (Common Era) as a substitute for "BC" (Before Christ) because they felt the older term wasn't fair to non-Christians. Many words originally described as "politically correct" have become commonly accepted; others have not. The term **politically incorrect** just means the opposite; for instance, the word "deaf" is now considered "politically incorrect."

Different left-wing groups and individuals can have opinions that range from just to the left of center, all the way over to the far left. Similarly, right-wing groups and individuals range from just to the right of center, all the way to far right.

In speaking of the "left" and the "right" in the United States today, however, we are not speaking of the extreme groups that exist at both ends of the scale. In the descriptions given above, the emphasis is on what is typical of left-wing and right-wing thought. It's possible that *nobody* would fully agree on everything said in the descriptions above because people do have different perspectives on life, politics and history. The descriptions are only meant to give some idea of this scale of perspectives on history.

MIDDLE OF THE ROAD: Middle-of-the-road people do not consider themselves either very far left or very far right, neither very liberal nor very conservative. Their opinions tend to be those that have been agreed upon by the history books they studied in school. They often have a mix of opinions depending on the issue, taking some from each side. They sometimes vote for a liberal politician in one election and a conservative politician in the next. Many have made an honest study of the issues and have decided that the mixed approach is the correct one. In an election, they vote for the person they like, regardless of political or historical perspective.

The main text you will use in your American history courses is *The History of US* by Joy Hakim. Her beliefs are in general somewhat to the left of the middle of the road. Her text was not chosen for this course because of her political beliefs, but because Ms. Hakim genuinely loves history, she loves people, and she loves the United States and the ideas that went into its creation. She makes an effort to be fair to both sides of any historical dispute, though she makes no attempt to hide her own opinions.

WHY STUDY HISTORY FROM MORE THAN ONE PERSPECTIVE?

If Ms. Hakim's textbook is so good, you may ask, why should you also be asked to read sections of a text that is even further to the left, and of a text that is more from the right?

One answer is that those books are good too, in their own way.

Howard Zinn (*A Young People's History of the United States*) did a wonderful job of finding many, many pieces of information that have often been left out of history books because the authors didn't know them, or else preferred to overlook them because they found them embarrassing. For instance, older American history books usually took the view that America was a wonderful country, and therefore everything Americans ever did in settling the country and expanding its borders was equally wonderful. Mr. Zinn's book shows in many ways that the early European explorers, settlers and pioneers in America did plenty of bad things, especially to the Native Americans and African Americans.

Some may feel that Zinn seems to have been unable to find anything that the more successful groups of Americans in those days did *right,* except for the ones who were rebelling or protesting about different things.

So we have Mr. Woods (*The Politically Incorrect Guide to American History*) to give us a different perspective. From Mr. Woods, we can get an idea of why some of the bad things happened the way they did, and sometimes why things that seemed bad might not really have been as bad as we think. However, some may feel Mr. Woods also sometimes seems to go overboard in excusing actions that we may think were very hard to excuse.

Reading both authors, we may be reminded again that very few things in life are absolutely one way or the other.

HISTORY IS IN THE STORIES

All of this brings us back to the concept of history as a story.

Both of these authors has a story to tell about America, although the stories are told from very different perspectives. Ms. Hakim has a third story to tell about America, one that is more joyful and more balanced than the other two, yet still leaves a lot of things out. And it is still *her* story, reflecting *her* opinions—it is not *the* story.

Many history textbooks pretend to tell *the* story—just the actual facts, without anyone's opinion being entered in. Unfortunately, there is really no such thing. Every history book is written by a live human being telling the story in his or her own way. There is really no way in which a writer can present information without communicating his or her opinions in the writing, whether that communication is open or hidden. And truly, there is no reason why writers ought to try to keep their opinions from showing, even though most of us prefer that they, at the same time, try to be as honest as they possibly can about any actual, proven, relevant data they have.

WHAT DOES IT MEAN TO BE A STUDENT OF HISTORY?

If there are so many differences of opinion among professional historians, how can students of history hope to make sense out of it all—and why should we even bother? What does it really mean to be a student of history?

Here are some ways we can make sense of it:

- We can do our best to establish as well as we can what the true facts are of any situation in history (or in current events, for that matter).

- We can make sure we have all of the relevant facts, or at least enough to understand the specific event or issue we are interested in.

- We can familiarize ourselves with some of the stories told by historians writing from different perspectives.

- We can ask ourselves which of these stories—if any—makes the most sense to us in helping us to understand events of the past *and* present.

MAKING SENSE OUT OF HISTORY

The records we have of the past provide at least the bare bones of the plot. The history that really matters, though, is right here in the present. For one thing, people are continually digging up new records that change the way we've always thought about certain events (they change our *perspective*).

You could think of history research as a "conversation," an exchange of ideas on past events. Events in the present affect the ongoing conversation among people who view the past from their different perspectives, but who are still trying (we hope) to come at the truth in the best way they know how. The story of history combines what facts we do have with the collection of stories that make up the conversation—as that conversation is happening right now.

The way we understand our shared past, the people, ideas and events that brought us to where we are now, is the key to our understanding of the present, and to our planning for the future.

We develop our own perspective, one that we are able to support with facts and logic, and that we think will make a good, truthful model for our actions in the present and the future.

We can expect that our version of the story will continue to change as we learn more and gain more experience along the way. We continue to check the accuracy of our facts from time to time, and we try to keep track of interesting new stories others are presenting. Most importantly, we apply the lessons we learn from our stories to our present actions. We use our understanding of history to help us act successfully in the present and to plan for the future.

Checks and Balances as Established by the U.S. Constitution

CHAPTER 6

CHECKS AND BALANCES AS ESTABLISHED BY THE U.S. CONSTITUTION

The writers of the Constitution hoped to prevent any part of government from getting too strong and doing things that weren't best for the country overall. If one part of the government got too powerful, the other two could act together to correct this.

The word **check** can be used to mean "to hold back or slow down or even stop." Two branches of government could *check* the third if it got too strong. With the branches able to check each other, the idea was to keep the government *balanced*. For this reason, the system in which the power of each branch of government is balanced by the others is called **checks and balances**.

Here's how it works. The first branch of the government makes the laws of the country. This is called the legislative branch, because to **legislate** means to make laws. This branch is also called **Congress**. Congress is made up of the House of Representatives and the Senate.

The second branch is the executive branch. An **executive** of a group runs the group and makes sure its rules are followed. This is what the executive branch does for the country. This branch is headed by the President of the United States. The President's job is to govern the country and to enforce the laws. The President is also Commander-in-Chief over the military forces of the country. **Commander-in-Chief** is the title of the top commander of the military forces of a nation, which includes all the soldiers who fight on land or sea or in the air.

The third branch of the government is the judicial branch. **Judicial** means "having to do with judges." This branch is headed by the Supreme Court. The Supreme Court has the job of deciding if the laws are correct and if they are being enforced correctly. A law that is in agreement with the Constitution is said to be **constitutional**. If a law does not agree with the Constitution, the Supreme Court may decide that it is **unconstitutional** and cancel it. It may also decide if a law is not clear and say exactly how the law should be used.

Here are some of the powers of each branch along with a few examples of how they check and balance each other.

Examples:

- A president can appoint a judge to the Supreme Court, but the Senate has the right to disapprove that appointment.

- A federal judge can be impeached and tried by the House of Representatives and Senate.

- The Legislative branch can pass a bill but the President can veto it. After the veto, the legislature can override the veto by a 2/3 majority of both the House of Representatives and the Senate. Then the bill becomes law despite the President's veto.

- A federal judge can decide if a law passed by the House of Representatives and Senate is constitutional or not.

LEGISLATIVE	EXECUTIVE	JUDICIAL
Congress makes the laws	Executive enforces the laws	Judicial interprets the laws
Passes laws	Signs bills into law but can also veto (but Legislative can override veto)	Decides if a law is constitutional
Can override Executive veto		Decides if an order from Executive is constitutional
Controls the federal budget	Spends money as Legislative directs	Determines how laws should be applied
Has taxing and spending power	Makes agreements and treaties with other countries (but treaties have to be approved by Legislative)	Determines how laws should be interpreted in order to be fair
Ratifies treaties made by the Executive		
Approves Executive appointments	Appoints judges and other officials in the federal government	
Power to impeach and try Executive officials and federal judges	Commander-in-Chief of armed forces	
Sole power to declare war		

CHAPTER 7

NOTES ON THE FILM
THE DAY AFTER TRINITY

CHAPTER 7

NOTES ON THE FILM
THE DAY AFTER TRINITY

THE MANHATTAN PROJECT—DEVELOPMENT OF THE ATOMIC BOMB

The first atomic bombs were developed during World War II in a top secret $2 billion government project called the "Manhattan Project."

The project was kept secret from Congress and the American public, and even from Harry Truman, the Vice President. The $2 billion price tag was an unheard-of sum for the times. If it had been known, it would undoubtedly have caused political troubles for the President and those concerned.

Dr. Robert J. Oppenheimer was the scientific director of the project. He was appointed to that job by General Leslie Groves, the senior army officer in charge of the project. These two men continued to play the leading roles in the drama that was the Manhattan Project.

The Day After Trinity (1980) is an excellent documentary on the Manhattan Project that features interviews with surviving participants of the Project, and contains movie footage from the 1930s and 1940s. It is 90 minutes long.

You may also wish to watch *Fat Man and Little Boy* (1989), a Hollywood movie dramatization of the Manhattan Project, featuring the major roles of General Groves and Dr. Oppenheimer. It gives a realistic feel for events surrounding the Manhattan Project from 1941 through 1945, when the bombs were used. It is 127 minutes long.

Another useful documentary is *Biography: J. Robert Oppenheimer—Father of the Atomic Bomb* (2000), an A&E biography. It covers Oppenheimer's entire life, including the Manhattan Project years, and the 1950s, when Oppenheimer was discredited and lost his security clearance. This documentary may be used as an additional reference. It is 50 minutes long.

QUOTES FROM *THE DAY AFTER TRINITY*

Oppenheimer: "The physicists have known sin and this is a knowledge which they cannot lose."

Robert Wilson: "The whole country was pulling together in a cause which even now I think was just. That is, the idea that Nazi Germany would win that war could have . . . [led] to a thousand years of Dark Ages, and everything we meant by civilization could come to an end. That seemed to me what the fight was about, or something close to that, and most Americans were in it just as hard as they could be."

I.I. Robbi: "It is amazing how the technology tools trap one. They are so powerful. The machinery had caught us in a trap and we were anxious to go."

Freeman Dyson (physicist and writer): "A Faustian bargain[3] is when you sell your soul to the devil in exchange for knowledge and power. And that of course, in a way, is what Oppenheimer did. There is no doubt. He made this alliance with the United States Army, in the person of General Groves, who gave him undreamed of resources, huge armies of people, and as much money as he could possibly spend, in order to do physics on the grand scale, in order to

---

3 Faust was a character of German legend who sold his soul to the Devil in exchange for knowledge. The story of Faust is the subject of much literature and music.

create this marvelous weapon. And it was a Faustian bargain, if ever there was one. And of course we are still living with the devil ever since. Once you sell your soul to the devil, there is no going back on it."

KEY FIGURES IN THE MANHATTAN PROJECT

It is recommended that you refer to this list as you study the Manhattan Project.

General Leslie R. Groves: In early 1942, Groves was the deputy to the chief of construction for the Army Corps of Engineers and was in charge of the construction of the Pentagon, the world's largest office building. He finished the project ahead of time and under budget. Against his objections, Groves was next assigned to head a top secret weapons project which became the Manhattan Project. Once he took on the project he was committed to making it succeed. In 1948 Groves retired from the army and became vice president of Remington Rand, an early computer company.

J. Robert Oppenheimer: Oppenheimer (called "Oppie" by his friends), was a brilliant scientist who was an expert in the newly emerging field of **quantum mechanics**, a field of physics that deals with sub-atomic energy particles/waves that do not obey the classical laws of physics. In October, 1942, Oppenheimer signed on with Groves and became Scientific Director of the Manhattan Project, after which he was involved with every step of the bomb development. After the war he resigned from the Manhattan Project, chaired the newly formed U.S. Atomic Energy Commission until he lost his security clearance, and taught theoretical physics at Princeton University. He became a vocal advocate for nuclear arms control.

[remainder are in alphabetical order]

Ralph A. Bard: Undersecretary of the Navy and member of the Interim Committee.[4] Bard wrote a confidential memo to Secretary of War Stimson on June 27, 1945, in which he proposed an alternative solution to using the atomic

---

4 The Interim Committee included high ranking politicians and military officers (including Groves). One of its purposes was to discuss the future of nuclear weapons.

bomb since Japan seemed close to surrender. He said that use of the bomb without warning was contrary to "the position of the United States as a great humanitarian nation."

Hans Bethe: German physicist who came to the U.S. in 1935 and taught at Cornell University. At Los Alamos he was the Director of the Theoretical Division and part of the senior management. During the 1980s and '90s he campaigned for the peaceful use of nuclear energy.

James F. Byrnes: Truman's chief political advisor and incoming Secretary of State in July, 1945, just before the test at Trinity. He was a major proponent for dropping the bombs on Japan.

Haakon Chevalier: French literature teacher at the University of California at Berkeley and a close friend of Robert Oppenheimer. When the Manhattan Project was underway, he told Oppenheimer that a Soviet agent was willing to convey secret data from the Manhattan Project to Soviet scientists (the Soviet Union was a U.S. ally at that time). Chevalier told Oppenheimer that he had told the agent he would not do so because he believed that decisions to transfer such information must be made at the highest levels. Later Oppenheimer reported the incident to Security in a confusing manner, which caused Chevalier to come under suspicion of being a spy and to lose his job.

A. H. Compton: physicist and director of the Metallurgical Laboratory at the University of Chicago (part of the Manhattan Project) during World War II. A.H. Compton was on the Scientific Panel[5] that recommended what should be done with the atomic bombs.

Ed Compton: Westinghouse physicist that Oppenheimer chose as his deputy director at Los Alamos. However, Ed Compton soon quit in protest over security restrictions that Groves was trying to impose. (Groves was trying to keep scientists from different areas of the project from sharing information so that no one but the top management would have the full picture of the project.)

---

5 The Scientific Panel was led by Oppenheimer, and also included A.H. Compton, Enrico Fermi and Ernest Lawrence.

Enrico Fermi: Italian physicist. In 1938, Fermi was forced to leave Italy because of the fascist regime under Mussolini. He moved to the United States. In late 1942 at the University of Chicago, Fermi and Szilard produced the first controllable chain reaction with uranium, which was the foundation for the atomic bomb. Afterwards Fermi moved to Los Alamos. He was a member of the Scientific Panel.

Richard Feynman: Physicist and mathematician who worked in the Theoretical Division under Hans Bethe and developed much of the mathematics behind atomic bombs. In the 1980s, Feynman was a key figure in determining why the *Challenger* space shuttle blew up. Many considered him to be second in genius only to Einstein.

Klaus Fuchs: German physicist and spy. In 1943, Fuchs began to work on the Manhattan Project. No one suspected that Fuchs had been transferring very detailed notes on the bomb project to a Soviet courier. His transfer of information greatly speeded up the Soviet atomic bomb effort. The Soviets exploded their first atomic bomb in Kazakhstan in August of 1949.

Kitty Harrison (**Kitty Oppenheimer**): married J. Robert Oppenheimer in 1940. She had previously been involved in Communist causes.

George Kistiakowsky: physicist and Russian refugee. In January, 1944, Kistiakowsky joined the Manhattan Project, replacing Seth Neddermeyer as head of the implosion program.

Col. John Lansdale: security and intelligence chief of the Manhattan Project.

Ernest Lawrence: Director of the University of California at Berkeley's Radiation Laboratory. Lawrence's research centered on nuclear physics. In 1929 he invented the **cyclotron**, a device for accelerating nuclear particles to very high velocities without the use of high voltages. The swiftly moving particles were used to bombard atoms of various elements, disintegrating the atoms to form, in some cases, completely new elements. Hundreds of radioactive forms of the known elements were also discovered. Groves considered him for the job of scientific director at Los Alamos, but Lawrence's own work was considered too valuable for him to leave Berkeley. Lawrence was a member of the Scientific Panel.

John Manley: experimental physicist at the Metallurgical Laboratories of the University of Chicago.

George C. Marshall: An Army general, U.S. Army Chief of Staff under Presidents Roosevelt and Truman, and a superb organizer. After the war he became Secretary of State under Truman and devised the Marshall Plan, which saved Western Europe from economic chaos.

Philip Morrison: physicist and group leader at Los Alamos; carried the plutonium bomb core to the Trinity test site.

Seth Neddermeyer: physicist in charge of implosion research in the Ordnance Division at Los Alamos until 1944, when he resigned.

Col. Kenneth Nichols: Groves' chief aide and troubleshooter during the Manhattan Project.

Frank Oppenheimer: Robert Oppenheimer's brother; physicist and Communist Party member.

Jacky Oppenheimer: Frank Oppenheimer's wife; Communist Party member.

Navy Capt. William S. ("Deke") Parsons: head of Ordnance Division at Los Alamos and part of senior management.

Isidor I. Rabi: Austrian physicist. At Los Alamos he worked on the development of radar and the atomic bomb. He then worked with Edward Teller on the hydrogen bomb, and later became involved with research into the peaceful uses of atomic energy.

Robert Serber: physicist and good friend of Oppenheimer. At Los Alamos he worked on the atomic bomb and wrote a primer on designing and building an atom bomb. After the bombs were dropped on Japan in 1945, he was with the first American team to enter Hiroshima and Nagasaki. They spent five months there assessing atomic bomb damage. Later he became an advocate of arms control.

Henry L. Stimson: Secretary of War under Presidents Roosevelt and Truman. He chaired the Interim Committee, which made recommendations to Truman on the use of the bombs. Stimson was one of Truman's closest advisors and was the one most intent on showing the Japanese no mercy.

Leo Szilard: Jewish German physicist (originally from Hungary) who was forced to flee Germany when Hitler came to power. He relocated to England, where he conceived the idea that a nuclear chain reaction was possible. In 1938, Szilard came to the United States. When he learned about the discovery of fission in Germany, he got Einstein to urge President Roosevelt to explore the development of an atomic weapon before Germany was able to. As a result of this request, Roosevelt initiated a small but secret uranium research project in 1939. In December 1942, Szilard and Fermi achieved the first controlled chain reaction at the University of Chicago. Later Szilard was a key figure in protests against the use of the atomic bomb.

Jean Tatlock: Robert Oppenheimer's mentally unstable girlfriend in the 1930s, and a Communist Party member. After Oppenheimer married Kitty Harrison, he continued to see Tatlock occasionally. When he was pressured to stop seeing her for security reasons, she committed suicide.

Edward Teller: Hungarian physicist. At Los Alamos he worked in the theoretical physics division. After World War II he was instrumental in the development of the much more powerful hydrogen bomb, which was a thousand times more powerful than the first atomic bombs. Oppenheimer opposed the project and refused to support it, saying there were no targets large enough to justify it. After Oppenheimer resigned from Los Alamos, Teller was put in charge of development of the hydrogen bomb and achieved the first successful test in 1952 by vaporizing an island in the South Pacific. Teller angered many physicists when he testified against Robert Oppenheimer at a "hearing" (actually a trial) in 1954 that led to Oppenheimer losing his security clearance.

James Tuck: British physicist at Los Alamos; involved in implosion experiments.

Stan(islaw) Ulam: mathematician and group leader at Los Alamos. Later worked with Teller on the hydrogen bomb.

Victor Weisskopf: Austrian physicist; group leader in theoretical physics at Los Alamos. Later he became a very strong advocate of nuclear arms control.

Robert Wilson: Cyclotron leader at Los Alamos. After the war he became active in efforts to ban the use of nuclear weapons.

Appendix

References for Chapter 5, Perspectives on History

The Age of Ideology: The 19ᵗʰ Century Philosophers, ed. Henry D. Aiken

Aristotle for Everybody, Mortimer Adler

None Dare Call It Conspiracy, Gary Allen

The Philosophy of Aristotle, ed. Renford Bambrough, Aristotle

Foreign Follies: America's New Global Empire, Doug Bandow

The Politics of Envy, Doug Bandow

The Italians, Luigi Barzini

From Dawn to Decadence: 500 Years of Western Cultural Life, Jacques Barzun

Selected Essays on Political Economy, Frédéric Bastiat

An Economic Interpretation of the Constitution of the United States, C.A. Beard

The Second Sex, Simone de Beauvoir

The Devaluing of America, William J. Bennett

The End of Ideology, Daniel Bell

Hirohito and the Making of Modern Japan, Herbert P. Bix

George Wythe of Williamsburg, Joyce Blackburn

The Closing of the American Mind, Allan Bloom

Freedom in Chains, James Bovard

A Decade of Revolution, 1789–1799: The Rise of Modern Europe, Crane Brinton

You Can Profit from a Monetary Crisis, Harry Browne

The Authoritarian Personality, Adorno and Frenkel-Brunswik

Reflections on the Revolution in France, Edmund Burke

The Myth of the Rational Voter, Bryan Caplan

Freedom and Virtue—The Conservative/Libertarian Debate, George Carey

The American Tradition, Clarence B. Carson

Professor Lord Acton, Owen Chadwick

The Constitution of the United States: A Study Guide, John Chambers

Thomas Jefferson, The Apostle of Americanism, G. Chinard

Hopes and Prospects, Noam Chomsky

Alexander Hamilton A Profile, ed. Jacob E. Cooke

Alistair Cooke's America, Alistair Cooke

Market Education, Andrew J. Coulson

Elementary Economics (textbook), Herbert J. Davenport

Don't Know Much About History, Kenneth C. Davis

Democracy and Education, John Dewey

Radicals for Capitalism, Brian Doherty

Who Rules America Now? William Domhoff

The Lessons of History, Will Durant

The Story of Philosophy, Will Durant

Rousseau and Revolution, Will and Ariel Durant

Friedrich Hayek, Alan Ebenstein

American Sphinx, The Character of Thomas Jefferson, Joseph Ellis

The Founding Brothers, Joseph Ellis

The Portable Emerson, eds. Carl Bode and Malcolm Cowley, R.W. Emerson

The Wretched of the Earth, Frantz Fanon

The War of the World, Niall Ferguson

Washington the Indispensable Man, James Thomas Flexner

The U.S. Constitution and Bill of Rights, Founders

The Autobiography and Other Writings, Benjamin Franklin

Collected letters of Benjamin Franklin, Yale University Press, Franklin

The Feminine Mystique, Betty Friedan

The Machinery of Freedom, David Friedman

The Next 100 Years, George Friedman

Free to Choose, Milton Friedman

REFERENCES FOR CHAPTER 5, PERSPECTIVES ON HISTORY

Uncommon Knowledge [video], Milton Friedman

Escape from Freedom, Erich Fromm

The Myth of the Robber Barons, Burton W. Folsom

The Landscape of History: How Historians Map the Past, John Gaddis

Understanding the Dollar Crisis, Percy Greaves

Descent into Slavery? Des Griffin

The Fourth Reich of the Rich, Des Griffin

Fathers of the Revolution, Philip Guedalla

A History of US [series of 10], Joy Hakim

The Federalist Papers, Hamilton, Madison, Jay

Text on Keynesian Economics, Alvin H. Hansen

The Constitution of Liberty, Friedrich Hayek

The Counter-Revolution of Science, Friedrich Hayek

The Essence of Hayek (ed. Nishiyama & Leube), Friedrich Hayek

The Road to Serfdom, Friedrich Hayek

Economics in One Lesson, Henry Hazlitt

Man vs. the Welfare State, Henry Hazlitt

The Worldly Philosophers, Robert Heilbroner

A Student's Guide to Economics, Paul Heyne

Mein Kampf, Adolf Hitler

The Leviathan, Thomas Hobbes

The True Believer, Eric Hoffer

Revolution for the Hell of It, Abby Hoffman

Masters of Deceit: The Story of Communism, J. Edgar Hoover

Benjamin Franklin: An American Life, Walter Isaacson

The Supreme Court in the American System of Government, Robert H. Jackson

Declaration of Independence, Jefferson and others

A History of the American People, Paul Johnson

Intellectuals, Paul Johnson

Profiles in Courage, John F. Kennedy

The General Theory of Employment, Interest and Money, J.M. Keynes

The Shock Doctrine, Naomi Klein

Peddling Prosperity, Paul Krugman

The Discovery of Freedom, Rose Wilder Lane

The Debate Over the Nature of Reality, Alan Larson and Jay Nunley

The Fair Tax Book, Neal Boortz, John Linder

Selections from The Second Treatise of Civil Government, John Locke

A Student's Guide to the Study of History, John Lukacs

The Prince and selections from The Discourses, Niccolo Machiavelli

The Armies of the Night, Norman Mailer

Principles of Macroeconomics (textbook), N. Gregory Mankiw

One-Dimensional Man: Ideology of Advanced Industrial Society, Herbert Marcuse

The Communist Manifesto, Friedrich Engels and Karl Marx

Das Kapital Book 1, Karl Marx

John Adams, David McCullough

The Chinese-Americans, Milton Meltzer

Gold, Milton Meltzer

On Liberty, John Stuart Mill

Utilitarianism, John Stuart Mill

The Austrian Theory of the Trade Cycle, Ludwig von Mises et al

Bureaucracy, Ludwig von Mises

Human Action, Ludwig von Mises

Selected Essays of Montaigne, trans. Fossio, ed. Crocker, Michel de Montaigne

The Spirit of Laws, Montesquieu

Lessons for the Young Economist, Robert P. Murphy

In Pursuit of Happiness and Good Government, Charles Murray

Our Enemy the State, Albert Jay Nock

Anarchy, State and Utopia, Robert Nozick

The Audacity of Hope, Barack Obama

Culture Warrior, Bill O'Reilly

Eat the Rich, P.J. O'Rourke

Common Sense, Thomas Paine

The Crisis, Thomas Paine

The Rights of Man, Thomas Paine

The God of the Machine, Isabel Paterson

The Life and Death of Lenin, Robert Payne

Confessions of an Economic Hit Man, John Perkins

The Republic, Plato

The Open Society and Its Enemies, Vol 1: The Spell of Plato, Karl Popper

Stalin: First In-Depth Biography, Edvard Radzinsky

Anthem, Ayn Rand

Atlas Shrugged, Ayn Rand

The Fountainhead, Ayn Rand

Philosophy: Who Needs It? Ayn Rand

The Romantic Manifesto, Ayn Rand

To Free or Freeze, Leonard E. Read

Ten Days That Shook the World, John Reed

Separating School and State, Sheldon Richman

Restoring the American Dream, Robert Ringer

America's Great Depression, Murray N. Rothbard

An Austrian Perspective on the History of Economic Thought, Rothbard

The Essential Ludwig von Mises, Murray N. Rothbard

For a New Liberty, Murray N. Rothbard

What Has Government Done to Our Money? Murray N. Rothbard

The Social Contract, Jean-Jacques Rousseau

How to Profit During the Coming Bad Years, Howard Ruff

History of Western Philosophy, Bertrand Russell

Citizens (French Revolution), Simon Schama

Child Abuse in the Classroom, Phyllis Schlafly

A Patriot's History of the United States, Schweikert and Allen

The Rise and Fall of the Third Reich, William L. Shirer

Walden Two, B.F. Skinner

Economics on Trial: Lies, Myths and Reality, Mark Skousen

The Power of Economic Thinking, Mark Skousen

On the Wealth of Nations, Adam Smith

American Government Cliffs Notes, Soifer et al

U.S. History I and U.S. History II: Cliffs Quick Review, Soifer and Hoffman

Basic Economics: A Citizen's Guide to the Economy, Thomas Sowell

Black Rednecks and White Liberals, Thomas Sowell

Classical Economics Reconsidered, Thomas Sowell

Knowledge and Decisions, Thomas Sowell

Race and Economics, Thomas Sowell

Inside the Third Reich, Albert Speer

The Man Versus the State and Six Essays, Herbert Spencer

A Nation of Victims, Charles J. Sykes

Walden and the essay "Civil Disobedience," Henry David Thoreau

Woman and the History of Philosophy, Nancy Tuana

Democracy in America, Alexis de Tocqueville

Philosophy: A Text With Readings, Manuel Velasquez

Perpetual War for Perpetual Peace, Gore Vidal

World Revolution, or The Plot Against Civilization, Nesta H. Webster

The Age of Analysis: The 20th Century Philosophers, ed. Morton White

Revolutionary Characters, Gordon S. Wood

American Government: A Complete Coursebook, Wood and Sansone

The Politically Incorrect Guide to American History, Thomas E. Woods, Jr.

Strictly for the Birds (satire on No Child Left Behind), R. B. Yockey

Whose America? Culture Wars in the Public Schools, Jonathan Zimmerman

A Young People's History of the United States, Howard Zinn